Produced by the Department of Publications
The Museum of Modern Art, New York

Hannah Kim, Business and Marketing Director
Don McMahon, Editorial Director
Marc Sapir, Production Director
Curtis R. Scott, Associate Publisher

Designed by Amanda Washburn
Production by Matthew Pimm
Printed and bound by Ofset Yapimevi, Istanbul

This book is typeset in Gunhill and Deccan.
The paper is 150 gsm Amber Graphic.

Children's Book Working Group: Samantha
Friedman, Cari Frisch, Sophie Golub, Emily Hall,
Hannah Kim, Elizabeth Margulies, Curtis R.
Scott, Amanda Washburn

With special thanks to Shahzia Sikander, for
sharing her work and her story

Thanks also to Hanna Barczyk, Janine
Cirincione at Sean Kelly Gallery, Naomi Falk,
Cerise Fontaine, Christopher Hudson, and Amy
Novesky

Shahzia would like to thank Azra, Sikander,
Mariam, Haroon, Akbar, and Alexander.

Library of Congress Control Number: 2020946483
ISBN: 978-1-63345-035-6

Published by The Museum of Modern Art
11 West 53 Street
New York, New York 10019
www.moma.org

Distributed in the United States and Canada by
Abrams Books for Young Readers, an imprint of
ABRAMS, New York
www.abramsbooks.com

Distributed outside the United States and Canada
by Thames & Hudson Ltd., London
www.thamesandhudson.com

Printed in Turkey

Photograph Credits

All photographs © 2021 Shahzia Sikander except
as noted

Flights of Fancy: © 2021 The Museum of Modern
Art, Department of Imaging and Visual Services.
Photograph by Robert Gerhardt

Gopi-Contagion: Photograph by Ka-Man Tse

How Shahzia Sikander
Became an Artist

Roots and Wings

Shahzia Sikander
and Amy Novesky

Illustrated by
Hanna Barczyk

The Museum of Modern Art
New York

A girl steps into a painting,
opens a door, enters a world, roams
from room to room.

A whole family lives here—
parents, sisters, brothers, grandparents,
aunts and uncles and cousins.
Dogs, rabbits, and cats, too.

The girl wanders and reads, observes and draws.
She paints a portrait of a girl.

I am the girl.
My home has many rooms.

The rooms are filled with words.
Ancient fables, Russian fairy tales,
poetry in English and in Urdu.
Bollywood films and American Westerns, too.

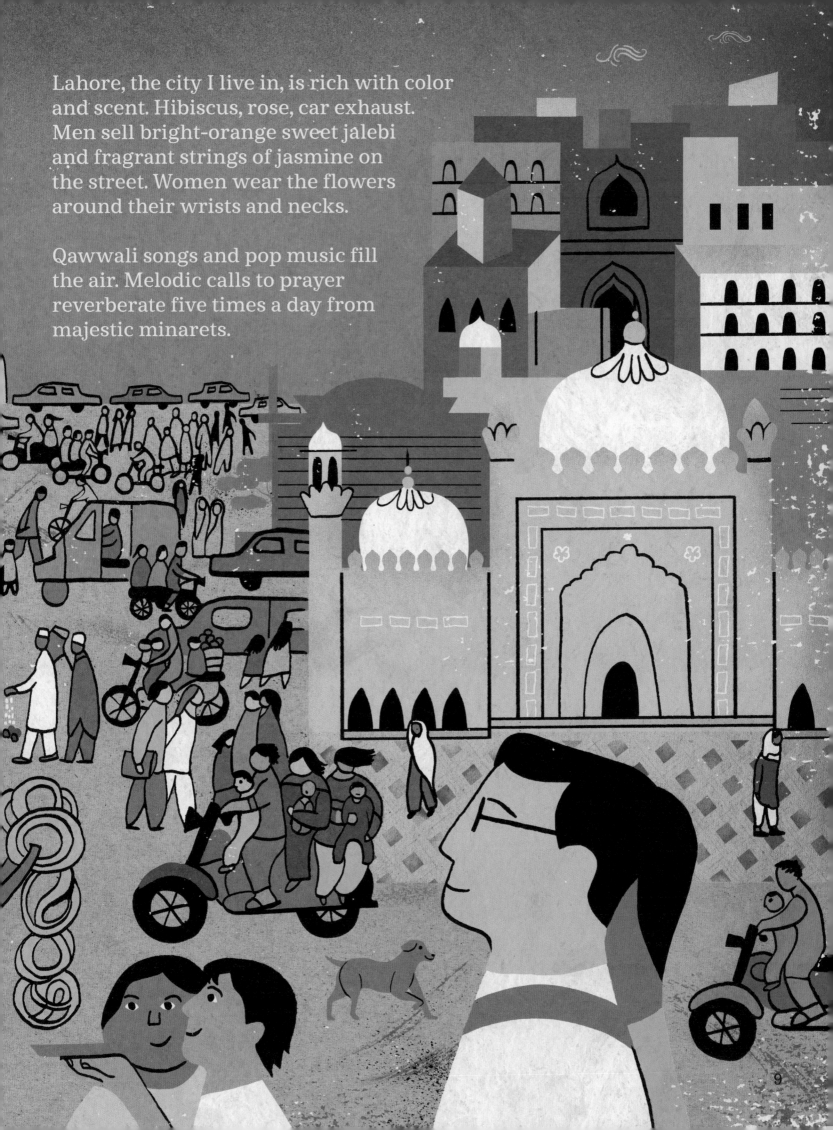

Lahore, the city I live in, is rich with color and scent. Hibiscus, rose, car exhaust. Men sell bright-orange sweet jalebi and fragrant strings of jasmine on the street. Women wear the flowers around their wrists and necks.

Qawwali songs and pop music fill the air. Melodic calls to prayer reverberate five times a day from majestic minarets.

We kids play cricket down in the streets.
I love to beat the boys at their games.
I skateboard. I fly kites. I climb trees.

My mother climbs trees, too.
She shakes the jamun branches. We catch the dark fruit
in bedsheets and eat it, our mouths turning purple.

Up on the roof, my cousins and I train pigeons.
We free the flock and watch it take off, wondering if
it will return.

From here I can see all the way to the horizon.

The sky is dotted with colorful shapes.
Not birds, not bats, but a swarm of kites.

On warm nights, my grandmother, my cousins,
and I sleep outside side by side on jute beds.
We watch stars spark and fireflies flash.
Their little lights and our heartbeats in sync.

12

When the city gets too hot, we take off, too, go north.
Quiet roads through pine forests cool as cathedrals.
Long winding roads to the mountains.
Time and space framed by my car window.

Once we traveled all the way to Rome!
Visited the Sistine Chapel, a kaleidoscope
of color and wonder.

Michelangelo and I share a birthday.

ITALY

Rome

BULGARIA

BLACK SEA

GREECE

TURKEY

MEDITERRANEAN SEA

TURKMENISTAN

SYRIA

IRAQ

IRAN

AFGHANISTAN

PAKISTAN

lahore

INDIA

BANGLADESH

ARABIAN SEA

BAY OF BENGAL

At school, I am quiet, shy, curious.

I am good at math. Numbers,
patterns, rhythms make sense.
Math is truth and beauty—
snowflake fractals, a constellation
of fireflies.

More even than math, I am good
at drawing. Birds—owls, hawks,
peacocks, pigeons—and people.

Drawing, like math, is a tool,
a way to figure out the world.

I study miniature paintings with a magnifying glass.
I see every detail: heroes and monsters, mythical birds
and beasts.
Miniature paintings are not small at all, but big.

I am an explorer discovering whole new worlds.
I am a heroine.

At art school, I train in miniature painting for hours and hours
with a master.
Such an ancient art is not considered cool, and it is hard work—
my first painting takes two years to make.

But it is here where I make the old new, I paint my own world.

I make the wasli paper, the glue from flour and water.
I paste them together, burnish it smooth with a seashell.
I color the paper with tea, render it radiant.

In hundreds of shells filled with a base of white,
I mix paint from pigment and ink.
So many pretty hues—pine tree green,
mountain blue, Sienna red.
Then, a single sable hair, the smallest gesture.

Art is my ritual,
my ticket to new
worlds.

23

Armed with a plane ticket and a suitcase full of paintings, I take off.
My family watches me, wonders if I will return.
I take my roots with me.
I land in America, but then I cannot leave.
My passport is not the right color.
My new country fears
the country I am from.

24

It will be nine whole years before I can go home again.
And so I work.
So much time to confront, to think, to imagine.
To draw, to paint, to create.

And then one day, a green card allows me to travel
once more.
I can fly around the world, roam—
I paint and show my work in Luang Prabang,
Honolulu, Sharjah, Sydney, Seville, Istanbul,
Berlin, Rome, Dhaka, Tokyo . . .

Now I live in New York City.
Here, in Times Square, worlds intersect.

The skyline fills with dark shapes. Not birds, not bats. Not kites.
The wings of my imagination.

So much time and space, I soar.

Artworks by Shahzia Sikander

Ready to Leave. 1997
Vegetable color, dry pigment, watercolor, ink, and
tea on wasli paper, 9⅞ × 7⁹⁄₁₆ in. (25.1 × 19.2 cm)
Whitney Museum of American Art, New York.
Purchase, with funds from the Drawing Committee

Pleasure Pillars. 2001
Vegetable color, dry pigment, watercolor, and
tea on wasli paper, 17 × 12 in. (43.2 × 30.5 cm)
Private collection

The Scroll. 1989–90
Vegetable color, dry pigment, watercolor, and tea
on wasli paper, 13 ½ × 63 ⅞ in. (34.3 × 162.2 cm)
Private collection

Flights of Fancy. 2009
Ink, gouache, and pencil on prepared paper,
15 × 11¼ in. (38.1 × 28.6 cm)
The Museum of Modern Art, New York.
Promised gift of Joel and Anne Ehrenkranz

Disruption as Rapture. 2016
HD video animation with 7.1 surround
sound, 10: 07 min.
Music composed by Du Yun, feat. Ali Sethi.
Animation by Patrick O'Rourke
Philadelphia Museum of Art. Commissioned
by the Philadelphia Museum of Art

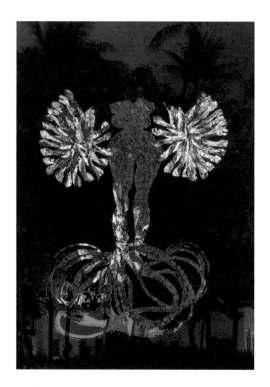

Unseen Series, #2. 2011–12
HD digital projection
Installation view, Shangri La, Museum of
Islamic Art, Culture, and Design, Honolulu

Arose. 2020
Glass mosaic, framed: 84 1/16 × 60 7/8 × 2 in.
(213.5 × 154.6 × 5.1 cm)
Minneapolis Institute of Art

Gopi-Contagion. 2015
HD video animation (color, silent), 3 min.
Installation view, Times Square LED billboards, New York,
as part of Midnight Moment, organized by Times Square Arts,
October 1–31, 2015

Shahzia Sikander

The Pakistani-American artist Shahzia Sikander grew up in Lahore, Pakistan, and moved to the United States in 1993. Her drawings, paintings, prints, mosaics, and animated films look at tradition, culture, and identity as ideas that change over time. Her interest in math and language led her to illuminated Indo-Persian books. She studied this vivid and detailed technique and its history—which began in Persia in the thirteenth century—as a teenager at the National School of Arts in Lahore. She takes this traditional genre as a starting point for exploring and examining new ideas.

The painting Shahzia examines through a magnifying glass on page 21 is *The Scroll*, which she painted in 1989–90, before she graduated from art school. (The whole painting is shown on pages 30–31). The work is done in the miniature technique, but instead of royal courts and battle stories, the scenes focus on physical and imaginative spaces. A ghostly young woman enters an imagined house and observes every room, where the activities of life are taking place: people playing, reading the newspaper, packing suitcases, cooking, eating, cleaning, and celebrating. As the woman observes, she takes us with her on a journey into time and space.

Shahzia's works have been shown in museums all over the world, and the collection of The Museum of Modern Art includes some of her prints, paintings, and drawings. She won a MacArthur Fellowship in 2006 and is considered a pioneer of neo-miniature painting.

For Shahzia, art has always been a ticket to life.

Shahzia with her grandparents, parents, uncle, aunt, siblings, and cousins in Lahore, 1984

Shahzia in her studio, New York, 2014

Glossary

Bollywood: India's Hindi-language movie industry. Bollywood films are often spectacular, with extravagant musical numbers.

Fractals: Complex and never-ending patterns found in math and nature. The way that new branches keep growing from tree trunks is an example of a natural fractal pattern.

Green card: A document that gives a person not born in the United States the right to live there permanently. Some people who hold green cards eventually become U.S. citizens.

Jalebi: A curly or pretzel-shaped sweet made of deep-fried flour soaked in syrup, popular throughout South and West Asia.

Jamun: A tree that bears sweet and sometimes-tart fruit also known as black plums.

Michelangelo: A sixteenth-century artist of the Italian Renaissance. One of his most famous works is the ceiling of the Sistine Chapel, in Rome, where more than three hundred figures illustrate stories from the Bible.

Minaret: A slender tower, built next to a mosque, from which devout Muslims are called to prayer five times a day.

Qawwali: Spiritual music sung by followers of the Sufi tradition, the mystical belief in Islam.

Urdu: The official language of Pakistan.